ANYONE'S GUESS HOW WE GOT HERE

Jack Perkins and Barrel Organ

ANYONE'S GUESS HOW WE GOT HERE

OBERON BOOKS
LONDON

WWW.OBERONBOOKS.COM

First published in 2017 by Oberon Books Ltd
521 Caledonian Road, London N7 9RH
Tel: +44 (0) 20 7607 3637 / Fax: +44 (0) 20 7607 3629
e-mail: info@oberonbooks.com
www.oberonbooks.com

A catalogue record for this book is available from the British Library.

PB ISBN: 9781786823403
E ISBN: 9781786823410

Cover design by Joe Boylan

Printed and bound by 4EDGE Limited, Hockley, Essex, UK.
eBook conversion by CPI Group (UK) Ltd, Croydon, CR0 4YY.

Characters

MAIN CHARACTER (MC) – F

OTHER CHARACTER (OC) – F

8-YEAR-OLD (8) – F

A play for two female performers. The two performers share three roles. See the table below of who is played by whom, and when.

	PERFORMER ONE	PERFORMER TWO
Scene One	Main Character	Other Character
Scene Two	Main Character	---
Scene Three	Main Character	8-Year-Old
Scene Four	---	8-Year-Old
Scene Five	Other Character	8-Year-Old
Epilogue	---	---

" – " at the end of a line indicates the speaker trailing off, or them being interrupted by the next line.

An empty line indicates a character responding, but not speaking. This, and a line-break within speech, is the shortest kind of pause. A longer pause is denoted by "Pause" in stage directions, and an even longer pause by "Longish Pause".

"/" indicates where lines should play over the top of each other. "[together]" indicates where lines are played simultaneously and in unison.

A question that doesn't end with "?" is still a question, but indicates a flatness of tone.

A show by Barrel Organ. Commissioned by and developed at Camden People's Theatre, with support from The Royal Exchange Theatre, Manchester, and Arts Council England.

First performed at ZOO Venues during the Edinburgh Festival Fringe from 13th to 28th August 2017 with the following cast:

Performer One
[Main Character, Other Character] – Bryony Davies
Performer Two
[Other Character, 8-Year-Old] – Rosie Gray

The same production was performed at Camden People's Theatre from 10th to 28th October 2017, and at Warwick Arts Centre, as part of the Emerge Festival, on 30th October 2017 with the following cast:

Performer One
[*Main Character, Other Character*] – Bryony Davies
Performer Two
[*Other Character, 8-Year-Old*] – Jade Ogugua

Text by Jack Perkins
Co-directed by Joe Boylan and Dan Hutton
Lighting Design by Lucy Adams
Sound Design by Kieran Lucas
Dramaturgy by Ali Pidsley

Barrel Organ are:
Joe Boylan
Bryony Davies
Rosie Gray
Dan Hutton
Euan Kitson
Kieran Lucas
Jack Morning-Newton
Jack Perkins
Ali Pidsley
Lulu Raczka
Katherine Thorogood

Notes on performance:

This is a play for two female performers. The cast cannot be any bigger or smaller than this. Productions must observe the scripted changes in role. See the prior table for guidance.

The performers are narrators and characters. They tell the story like external observers, and they also embody the characters. The transition between the two states is sometimes a slow bleeding-in-effect, and at other times a snap.

Longer stage directions are printed at the end of the text. They are a partial record of the production by Barrel Organ. When these moments occur see "turn to page..." references in the main-body of the text.

SCENE ONE

MC   Two people, in a car.

OC   Driving down an A-road. At night.

MC   Heading to a funeral.

OC   In the middle of the midlands.

MC   Entering Robin Hood country.

OC   The home of Major Oak.

MC   The thousand-year-old tree.

OC   Three trees sprouting from one base.

MC   Tangled up in each other.

OC   As thick as a –

MC   Tree trunk.

OC   Redundant comparison.

MC   It looks like three sisters growing old in the place they were born.

OC   Fuck off does it.

            No, it looks like three witches sealed in bark.

MC   If you take trees as female. Mother Nature, all that.

OC   It's so old, the branches are held up by scaffolding.

MC   To stop it collapsing under its own weight.

OC   It's being preserved.

1

MC	It's not yet dead.
OC	They say this is the tree he used as a hide-out.
MC	The man in the green tights.
OC	Where they buried the loot.
MC	Before it was re-distributed to those who needed it.
OC	You know the saying.
MC	No. Which one.
OC	Take from –
MC	Take from the rich.
OC	Give to the poor. That tree has seen it all go down.
MC	If you believe the stories.
OC	You can choose to.
MC	Here's one.
OC	Another story.
MC	Happening now. Imagine.
OC	They're driving over what was once Sherwood Forest. Where the most famous story of taxation happened.
MC	Might have happened.
OC	There's no off-shore tax-haven in the woods, with a bow and fucking arrow in your face.
MC	Come on, back to them.

OC	The two people, in the car. They're heading to the funeral. For –
MC	No.
	Pause
	I mean, not yet.
OC	Heading to a funeral –
MC	Before that.
OC	Alright.
MC	Tomorrow, the funeral. Tonight, they're making a detour. To a house –
OC	A terrace –
MC	In a market-town. Where she grew up.
OC	The one in the front passenger seat.
MC	Where she spent the first eight years of her life.
OC	She hasn't been back since.
MC	In the morning she's meeting her family.
OC	She didn't tell them about the detour to the childhood home.
MC	Her brothers were too young. They won't remember.
OC	Her mum, and her –
MC	Picking a scab. No. Just her.
OC	And me? I'm at the steering wheel.

3

MC	You're the driver. The one I confided in. You pushed me into doing this.
OC	We're neighbours.
MC	Or we share a house.
OC	We volunteer at the Library.
MC	We write on a message board online.
OC	We drink at the pub.
MC	In a club.
OC	On a night out.
MC	We went to a protest.
OC	Or we work for the same catering agency.
MC	We're school friends.
OC	From childhood.
MC	I knew you back then.
OC	I have a car.
MC	I owe you for this.
OC	I offered to help.
MC	I have something to do at my old house, something unfinished.
OC	And, the game?
MC	I spy?

OC   No.

MC   Yellow Car.

OC   Piss off.

            I told you to stop doing that.

MC   Guess what time it is.

OC   Um. 21:15.

MC   Who says –

OC   I'm being specific. Quarter past nine. Your guess.

MC   Oh. Oooo. Fuck. Fuckfuckfuckfuck. Half ten.

OC   Locking-in your answer.

MC   It is –

            Phone's dead. What's the dashboard say. Press
            the button.

OC   It's wrong. Changes every time I switch the engine
            on.

MC   Six-thirty-seven. No, that's not right.

OC   What I said.

            Pause

MC   Are you alright for directions? I can't give you any
            more.

OC   Memorised the route, told you. Didn't need you
            to keep checking.

5

Longish Pause

MC   You're drifting. Do you need to close your eyes for a bit?

OC   I'm not, and no.

MC   I'm watching the lines in the road.

OC   I'm fine. I have you to keep me on edge.

Longish Pause

Can you move your leg? In the way of the stick.

MC   Yeah. Sorry. Another one? A-Z. How about 'things you owe'. Go.

OC   Alright. Album, U2, 'The Joshua Tree', –

MC   Cringe.

OC   I never gave back to my cousin. They were good then.

MC   Back to it. B.

OC   Birthday present, for my mum. Said she didn't mind, that seeing me was enough. Definitely a lie.

MC   Don't need the running commentary.

OC   Fine. C, Council Tax. Late on that. D, Debt. Does that count?

MC   That's not the point of the – /

Yeah fine, that counts.

OC	/ M&S card I'm still paying off, phone contract, the parking fine I got because you took too long.
MC	I'm going to cover that. Go on. E.
OC	Um. Pass. F. Oh, Fran. / She gave me a lift when the car broke down.
MC	/ No, you can't –
OC	Still haven't returned the favour.
MC	No, no passes. It's supposed to be –
	That's the challenge.
OC	G.
	No. I've gone blank.

They play another car-game: 'Shag, Marry, Kill' or 'Would you rather'. The questions asked are new for each performance. OC asks MC. MC answers and then poses a question for OC. OC however doesn't answer, as she becomes aware that they're approaching their exit from the A-road.

Here we go. It's this exit isn't it.

MC	Oh.
OC	Quickly.
MC	Uh.
OC	I'm going to miss it.
MC	Yeah, yeah, turn here.

Pause

OC   One more?

MC   Go on.

OC   Let's do *Thelma and Louise*.

MC   The end?

OC and MC recreate the ending of the film 'Thelma & Louise'. Their accents should be as close to the-real-thing as can be achieved. However, it is their own re-creation of what happens. They've played this game many times. Small changes and misquotations have crept into their re-enactment. Their quoting of the film has stopped being accurate, and become something different

OC   The car is parked-up. They're looking out.

MC   *[Louise]* Whaddya know, we made it. The goddamn Grand Canyon.

OC   *[Thelma]* Innt it just. I don't know – beautiful?

MC   *[Louise]* Yeah. Something else entirely.

OC   Then. Sound of helicopter blades. And it rises, over the verge.

MC   It's –

Arrrgghh. Man from *Reservoir Dogs*, and his name is –

OC   Yes.

MC   Harvey Keitel.

OC	He's caught up with them.
MC	
OC	Go on.
MC	Oh yeah. The helicopter, um, whips up dirt, their hats fly off.
OC	They turn the car around.
MC	And in the distance a squadron of police cars –
OC	Sirens blaring.
MC	Cutting them off.
OC	Police cocking rifles.
MC	Loading magazines. Aiming their sights on the car.
OC	*[Thelma]* Jesus. They look like an army.
MC	*[Louise]* All this fuss?
OC	The helicopter lands.
MC	Harvey Keitel and –
	Stephen Tobolowsky step out. Knew that one.
OC	*[Hal]* You can't shoot those girls. What're ya doing with all these guns pointing at 'em?
MC	*[Max]* These women are armed Hal, and dangerous. You better fall down. I can have you on desk duty like that.

9

OC	[Trooper with megaphone] Place your hands where we can see them. If you fail to obey this command, we will consider it an act of aggression against us.
OC	[Thelma] Louise, what're you doing?
MC	[Louise] I'm not going down like this.
OC	[Hal] You gotta de-escalate the situation Max. How long Max, how –
	Fuck, um, I mean –
	[Hal] How many times this woman gonna be fucked over?
MC	[Max] You pull yourself together. Listen to me. The boys know what they're doing. Don't make me regret letting you tag along.
OC	[Hal] Gawddammit.
MC	[Trooper with megaphone] I repeat, cut the engine and put your hands in the air.
OC	Then, then –
	A guitar riff.
MC	Swelling underneath. The sun in the desert.
	MC and OC sing / "da-da-da" the melody. They may then laugh at themselves
OC	[Thelma] Stop it, hey, stop. Listen. Let's not get caught.
MC	[Louise] Whadda ya mean?
OC	[Thelma] Let's keep driving.

10

MC	*[Louise]* You're not talking sense.
OC	*[Thelma turns her head forwards, looking out, and then back to Louise]* Go.
MC	*[Louise breathes. Smiles. Laughs.]* Thelma, are you sure?
OC	*[Thelma]* Yeah. Hit it.
MC	*[together]* Kiss for good luck.
OC	*[together]* Kiss goodbye.
OC	Huh?
MC	They kiss to say thank you.
OC	They kiss to hype themselves up, for what they're about to do.
MC	All of those things, all at once. The car starts to move.
OC	Tyres spin up dust.
MC	Slow motion of Harvey Keitel chasing after them.
MC	*[together]* They hold hands.
OC	*[together]* They hold hands.
OC	Snap zoom-in on their hands.
MC	Foot full-down on the pedal. Floors it.
OC	Flying off the edge.
MC	*[together]* White-out.

OC	*[together]* White-out.
OC	We don't see them fall.
	Pause
MC	You know there's a deleted scene? An alternate ending.
OC	No.
MC	We see them fall. Down the cliff.
OC	Piss off.
MC	No guitar. This country song with electric organ. Something about 'flying' and 'full speed ahead'.
OC	That's –
	Criminal. They were going to use that?
MC	I don't know.
OC	Fucking hell. Go on. They don't show them on the ground –
MC	No, no.
OC	Some dignity.
MC	The car disappears behind the rocks. Harvey Keitel runs up to the edge. The helicopter goes down after them. Close-up on his face. And then they cut to a shot from earlier. Their car again, but on the road. Driving off into the horizon.
OC	That's so –
	Like someone who hates the film did that.

MC   I'll show you later.

OC   No, don't. Then it'll be there, every time I watch it.

MC   They must have test-screened it.

OC   The negative underneath.

MC   The last five minutes change the whole story.

OC   How'd tonight get cut together, us?

MC   Saying we're like them, at the end?

OC   I didn't think the midlands had a Grand Canyon.

MC   No, seriously. Is that what I'm doing to myself, going back.

OC   Depends. Is this Falling or Whiting-Out?

MC   I don't know.

            The rest of the drive is in silence.

OC   As far as we know.

MC   Until they pull up in the back street.

OC   Behind her old home.

MC   Beside the garden-fence.

OC   Tell them why, tell them what happened.

MC   When she was eight, they were evicted. Not quite evicted, almost. They sold the house just before the final notice. They'd got months behind. When her dad stopped working and her mum couldn't

	support them all. They moved into rented and they were back to zero.
OC	Back to zero doesn't feel like back to zero though, does it.
MC	On the last night of residency, she left something.
OC	It was a stuffed bear she'd had since she was born.
MC	Or a tube with all her baby teeth.
OC	A pen that lit-up and played Jingle Bells.
MC	Or the first pound coin she was ever given.
OC	She thought she was helping.
MC	It wasn't an accident.
OC	It was on purpose. In a hidden place.
MC	Now she's back.
OC	Before the funeral.
MC	To reclaim it.
OC	The funeral for –
MC	Her dad. For her dad.
OC	What she left behind, all those years ago. It's eaten up her memories of him.
MC	She tries to see his face. Not in pictures. In motion, in her head. But she can't. He's blanked out. The trying just made it worse. The emptiness. Where he should be, is this thing.

OC	This thing she can't forget.
MC	Lost in the dark, and waiting.
OC	Tonight, she finds it. And she puts it to rest.
MC	With him.
OC	She'll see him again.
MC	And she'll say goodbye.
OC	We fill in the story.
MC	The blank spaces.
OC	To end that story, and start the one that comes after.
MC	She steps out the car.
OC	I say: don't disturb more than you have to.

MC

I'm feeling along the fence, for a loose panel. Imagine. The gap I slipped through, to come and go as I pleased. That I was told over and over: "this is not a door, you're not to use it as one". But it was, and I did. It slides open. I'm squeezing through, picking up splinters in my hair. I'm in the garden of the house I grew up in. It's gone wild. Weeds up to my knees. In the overgrown, there's a clearing. Concrete. Weathered glass. Shredded tarp. The junk spreads out like a dusty finger-print of what used to be here.

The shed. I remember that summer, captured in Dad's photo-album. My brothers, splashing in a paddling pool. None of them wearing any clothes. I re-make the images in my head. Me at the top of the slide, about to leap into the water. The pushchair weighed down by shopping. Mum shouting, telling us to stop pissing about and pack the pool away. Her face: sunburn and anger.

What happened next isn't in any of the photos. I locked the shed, turned my back on it and fell over my brothers. The three of them on their hands and knees. Heads disappearing underneath. I'd never seen them so quiet. They'd wind each other up, but they couldn't stand to be apart. They bit and pinched when they were together. And howled for each other when they weren't. I didn't ask why. I didn't want to break it, whatever had them so transfixed. I got down and I looked.

In the dark, way way back where the shed meets the hedge, there was this moving pile of orange fur. Four, then six, eight, ten green eyes looking back at us. No one was breathing. We didn't reach out our hands. Or make the noise you do to call a cat over. The babies jostled, to find a warmer spot under the bigger fox. Silent as we were. Not breaking our stare.

We didn't tell Mum about it. Before we went inside, my brothers looked at me, and I think it was the same look we gave those foxes. We made a promise. To not bring the grown-ups into it. To let them stay for as long as they needed. We called space-under-the-garden-shed 'Foxland', and allowed the travellers shelter. But then, you're a kid. It's an age from Monday to Saturday. We checked on them the next day. And then we forgot. The foxes might've been there days. It might've been months.

And now it's been years. And Foxland has been torn up. And I'm back in the garden, approaching the door. Number 26. I'm turning the handle. I'm going in.

It stinks. More black mould than there is wall. It's like my mouth is full of soil, like being buried alive. Sheets of wallpaper curled on the floor. Think of the estate agent trying to talk it up now. The property boasts indoor wild-life. No up-keep necessary. A modest increase in the asking price. We sold it for half what we paid for it. Where does all that go. It doesn't just disappear.

It's the bit of the night between the noise. Water rising below my skin. I'm climbing the stairs, holding my breath. The door on the left. Into my childhood bedroom. My eyes are swimming in it. Same ratty carpet shifts underneath my feet. Still not been tacked-down. In the corner, the carpet pulls back. And a floorboard lifts straight out from the rest. Like the fence. Like under-the-shed. They found me. Whole other worlds, in the gaps, in the cracks underneath my feet.

In that hole, I buried something. I thought one day we'd come back for it. Like children think. We'd go away. We'd take our punishment. And then, I would tell my parents what I'd done. And we'd drive all the way here. We'd be allowed to stay. It was a deposit to guarantee our return. It has. I just got the time wrong, and the number of us.

Pause

I lost him.

And he's down here.

I find it, I find him. I find it, I find him. I can pull him out. I can bring him back.

MC searches for the object. Stage Direction One, turn to p.45

Ah fuck. Fuck. It's gone. I'm too late.

Remember then. What happened. I was eight. And I went to bed. And I waited for the lights to go out.

SCENE THREE

8	Hello.
MC	Jesus, don't sneak up on me like that.
8	What time is it? Are we going now?
MC	Um.
8	It's still dark.
MC	
8	You're not my dad.
MC	No.
8	
MC	What's your name.
8	Laura.
MC	Fucking hell.
8	Don't swear.
MC	Am I in your bedroom Laura?
8	Yes.
MC	Right. Okay.
	Pause
8	Are you alright.
MC	Yeah. What.

8	You were shouting.
MC	Sorry. Did I wake you up.
8	I wasn't sleeping.
MC	I didn't see you.
8	You're not a very quiet burglar.
MC	No, that's –
	I'm not.
8	What're you doing then?
MC	I'm looking for something.
8	Sounds like a burglar.
MC	Oh god, I'm out of my fucking depth here kid.
8	We haven't got anything for you to take. It's all in the van.
	Pause
MC	You're leaving tomorrow then?
8	Yeah. We have to.
MC	You're staying with your mum, while Dad's on the waiting list.
8	Who are you?
MC	This morning. The van pulled up in the street. On the side it said –
8	"CAUTION WORKING DOGS".

MC	It wasn't the van you were waiting for. Even with the doors shut, you could hear them whining. You counted the seconds between their calls. Like thunder and lightning. You wondered what a 'working dog' looked like.
8	I knocked on the window. I asked the man in the front to let me see.
MC	He laughed, but you were serious.
8	He unlocked the back –
MC	But he didn't turn the key fast enough.
8	The alarm.
MC	The dogs panicked. Two German Shepherds.
8	They were crying. I whispered to them.
MC	Put your hand up to the cage.
8	I tried to let them out.
MC	The man pulled you back.
8	He screamed at me.
MC	Said you could've lost your fingers.
8	The vans can't take everyone away. Laura?
MC	Yeah.
8	What happens to us? If you've come back, it must be really really bad. Does Dad –

MC	He's –
	That's not for you to worry about.
	Pause
8	What have you come to do?
MC	I –
8	You're going to stop the house being taken.
MC	No.
8	We'll seal the doors shut.
MC	Stop interrupting.
8	We can make a daisy-chain of bike-locks and –
MC	Shut up.
8	Then what?
MC	You know the hole.
8	Under the floorboard.
MC	Yeah. What we put down there. It's gone.
8	Don't know what you mean.
MC	What.
8	I haven't put anything down there.
MC	This is the last night. That's what you do.
8	But I haven't.

MC	It's me. You can't lie to me.
8	I'm not.
MC	Don't mess me about.
8	Okay, then let's look again.
MC	You don't know.
8	Maybe, maybe its deeper in the house.
MC	This is hopeless.
8	I'll get a torch.
MC	I can't stay.
8	No. No.
	You're not going to help us.
MC	There's nothing to be done.
8	We can change what happens.
MC	Come on. Look, out there

Longish Pause. In the story, MC forces 8 to look out the window, to see that they are in MC's present and not 8's. In the performance, 8 makes eye-contact with everyone in the audience

8	It's all old.
MC	It's been years.
8	It smells.
MC	Cover your mouth.

8	Laura.
MC	Have you been waiting here, this whole time.
8	No. Laura.
MC	A fucking ghost.
8	I'm not.
MC	You're wrong.
8	This is a nightmare.
MC	I didn't come for you.
8	Stop it. Dad.
MC	What're you doing.
8	Dad, Dad, DAD. DAD.
MC	He won't answer. He's not coming.

8 continues to call for her dad. MC holds 8 by the shoulders. 8 struggles. MC grips her tighter, 8 is flailing now. MC pins 8 down on the ground

8	Please don't hurt me. Please please please don't.
MC	I won't. I'm not.
8	I'm sorry, I'm sorry, I'm sorry, I'm sorry.
MC	Stop freaking out.
8	You're crushing me.
MC	Why are you here.

8	I can't breathe. I can't breathe, I can't breathe.
MC	Alright, I'm off.
	MC releases 8
MC	I lift her back onto her feet.
8	The bedroom door is open.
MC	Her pyjamas are wet. She's pissed herself.
8	I'm closer to the door than she is.
MC	She's too real.
8	I take my chance. I run.
MC	She's halfway down the stairs before I do anything. I follow after.
8	I don't turn back. I'm moving so fast I'm falling.
MC	The kid's out the back-door, into the garden. Door left swinging behind her. I step through.
8	I'm not in the garden.
MC	No, hang on –
8	I'm in a shop.
MC	Stop. I'm lost.
8	The automatic doors slide closed.
MC	This isn't right. Where's –
8	I stop running.

MC	I'm not in the garden. I'm in Dad's living room.
8	She's gone. The monster pretending to be me.
MC	The private flat that was supposed to be temporary. That became his home, after waiting on the council list and not getting anywhere. Where Dad lived, after Mum's care stretched until it broke. Where he died. Enough space for him, not the rest of us. We stopped over when he could take us. Could see the embarrassment on his face, when he couldn't provide.
	The blinds are drawn. The sound of someone sleeping, breathing.
	There he is. I've found him. On the floor, wrapped up in duvet.
8	I'm in Cash Converters. Standing at the till, hands on the jewellery cabinet. Inside are Mum's rings. Pawned to pay for the van. Said she's coming back for them, when we're settled in. Smiled like grown-ups do when they're lying. The shop is small, but it's rammed full. On the shelves is us. I mean it's all ours. Coats and building blocks and photo albums and DVDs and board games and pots and pans. Not in the van. It's been taken here and unloaded.
MC	I don't speak. I barely breathe. I watch him. The duvet expands and contracts. I can't see his face.
8	And baby-grows and hoovers. And that golf club Dad bought off the market. It's everything we ever owned, we ever lost, used, broke, replaced, threw away. And where there's no more room on the shelves, black bags piled on black bags in the aisles.

MC	By his head, the radio. On the screen, it says SEARCHING FOR SIGNAL. Then SIGNAL FOUND. Then VOL MAX.
8	Dad's favourite record is spinning on a deck. The one with the screaming face on the cover. The needle drops when I look at it.
MC	That song by King Crimson is playing.
8	The sound is coming out every speaker.
MC	The noise is so deep, the vibration is shaking the air in my lungs.
8	The walls are moving.
MC	It's this thing he'd do for his pain. When it'd flare up. He'd lay down and he wouldn't be able to lift himself up again. The kind of pain when someone's not there. Trying to speak to them, like calling long distance. To take himself away from the pain, he'd turn the radio up really loud. So loud it's chipping away at his skin. I think it was all the sensation. Like drowning it out, he'd stop feeling. And then he'd be able to sleep. A temporary solution. It'd go for a while, but it'd always come back.
8	The shop is caving in. DVDs fly out of their cases and shatter against the wall. Bin bags crushed under falling shelves. Spaghetti hoops, shampoo, sun cream, blackcurrant squash pour out. The bags glug empty. I grab whatever's closest. To take it back. The golf club, a photo album. I run for the entrance.
MC	The duvet wriggles. Dad makes this moaning noise. He's trying to tell me something. I say: oh, sorry, I thought you were asleep. The duvet unfolds, and

an old man steps out of it. He's not Dad. I say to him, I say it to her, to the house: you've tricked me.

8   I stop at the jewellery cabinet. I hammer my fists against the glass. It doesn't budge. I drop the photos. I raise the club.

MC   The man's wearing Dad's work uniform. The factory where he packaged frozen-food. The duvet opens, and another man gets out. They're rocking and nodding their heads. More of them, coming out of this bottomless duvet, and they're dancing.

8   A shelf falls by my head. It knocks over the cabinet, shatters the glass. I lose sight of Mum's rings. Turn my back and run.

MC   The men are filling up the room. They're dancing even harder. Arms flailing. They're blocking my way out. I'm weaving between them, they're kicking my shins. I shove them back, they step onto the duvet. It rolls open and they're knocked off their feet, as more men climb out.

8   The automatic doors ding open.

MC   They're falling over. They're piling on the floor. And they're still dancing. I stamp on their fingers, kick loose their grabbing hands. I reach the door, I slam them in behind me.

8   The music stops. I'm back in my room.

MC   I'm in the hallway, at the top of the stairs. Outside my old bedroom.

8   No more intruders. No more exploding shops. No more.

MC   I won't stop until I find him. Throw everything at me, I'll –

               No, I can't. I can't.

8   She's outside. Sounds like screaming. I'm still holding the golf club.

MC   I open the door.

8   I see a foot. And then a head.

MC   I step into my childhood bedroom.

8   I close my eyes and swing the club as hard as I can.

8 kills MC. Stage Direction Two, turn to p.46

SCENE FOUR

I hit. She falls down. I let go.

It's her. Me. She doesn't get up.

I wait, to be sure. I turn on the light. I get closer, and I look at her face. She's not a monster. Her eyes are red, puffy. She looks scared. I didn't mean –

I had to make her stop.

I won't cry. I don't cry. The house is still. It's stopped moving. Doors don't lead elsewhere.

In the corner, the carpet is pulled back. A floorboard is propped against the wall. Where she was digging. I don't know what she buried under there. If she did, I didn't do it yet. I reach into the dark, and pull up more floorboards on either side. The wood crumbles in my fingers. It's rotting. Whatever it was, it's gone. It's lost.

I drag her further into the room. I try not to hurt her. I don't want to put her through anymore. I plant her feet in the hole. I fill the space under the floorboards with her. Gently lower her head.

I kneel, get right in her ear, and say: when we paid it off, it should've been finished. We should've been saved. And here you are. What did it do to you? I'm going to finish it. I'm going to lift the curse. I'm going to take over for you. I'm going to take over for you. I'm going to make this house nothing. I'm going to pull this whole thing down.

I march down the stairs. The mould runs off the walls and on to the floor. I'm out the back-door, into the garden. The windows black-out. The door squeezes shut so tight it's creaking. The whole building is heaving. It's trying to scare me. Because it's a cornered animal. It's terrified of what I'm going to do. I put my hand out, hold it steady. I shut my eyes. The glass in the window-frame screams. And then I get to work.

In the living room, I strip the wallpaper. I take out the sofa, the table, the armchair. As much as I can move, as much as I can carry. I make a pile in the garden. In the clearing, where the shed used to be.

I find bottles under the kitchen-sink. I douse the walls in the hall, and up the stairwell. I bleach the mould and wipe until the black comes clean. The sun comes up. I shuffle out the fridge-freezer, the washing machine. Stack them at the base. I unscrew the cupboard doors and add them to the pile.

In the bathroom, I tear down the shower curtain. I peel the sealant from round the bathtub. I scratch away the grouting, fill the tub with tiles. I push the bath down the stairs.

In the master bedroom, I jump up and down on the bedframe until it snaps. I throw it out the window piece by piece. Night falls. I bleed the radiators. Let the water run into the carpet and down the stairs.

Outside, I set the ladder against the wall. I pull down the guttering. I pick out every roof-tile. Throw them onto the pile. Days are running into each other. I pull ivy from the walls. I use a blow-torch to burn the weeds in the cracks. I fill a bucket with water and wash the windows. Black tears run down the glass.

Stage Direction Three, turn to p.47

In the basement, I turn off the water supply, switch off the mains electricity, remove the fuse-box. I take a sledgehammer and smack into the walls. I expose the wires. I lose my balance. I pick myself up. I keep swinging until I see the pipes. I pull them out like loose threads on a jumper. I don't tire.

I go back to my bedroom. I'm cut and bruised and burnt and filthy. Weeks have passed. It might've been years. The floorboards have turned to compost. The hole remains. I plunge my hands in deep. In the spot we keep returning. And lift a skeleton out of the soil. Carry it on my shoulders. I don't let it touch the ground. There's no more room in the garden. Can't see the grass for the tower of wreckage. It's as tall as the house. I scale the pile on my hands and knees. The skeleton on my back. Stand on the unsteady top. And lay the bones among the breakage.

I descend from the peak. I take a jerrycan. I show it to the house. I drench the bottom of the pile in petrol. Ignite the blowtorch. And up it goes.

The smoke is black. Charcoal black. Black like black mould black.

I watch the pyre. I don't know what I expected to feel. It illuminates my face. But there's no heat.

It's on fire. But it doesn't burn.

The flames don't spread, the house doesn't catch alight. It's contained. As if I achieved nothing.

The fridge-freezer falls to one side. And out of the rubble crawl a family of foxes. Glowing orange. They saunter past me and stop at the fence. The biggest fox lifts the smaller ones by the scruff of the neck and drop them through the gap. Clocks me. Waits. Disappears after them.

It's not enough. It doesn't end here. I turn away. I step through the gap in the fence. The light goes out, but it continues to burn, inside my ears. Something else, something more. Cinders in my stomach. I walk onto the next street. A car ahead flashes its headlamps. It pulls up next to me.

SCENE FIVE

OC   Get in, get in. You got your belt on?

8   Uh-huh.

OC   Which way am I going at the roundabout?

8   Second exit.

OC   You're covered in shit.

8   It was a mess in there.

OC   It stinks.

8   Open a window.

OC   You were gone ages.

8   Yeah.

OC   I was just about to check on you.

8   You waited all this time.

OC   Uh, yeah, course I did. You alright.

8   Yeah. Fine.

OC   Will you show me?

8   What.

OC   Did you find what you needed?

8   No.

OC   Right. I'm sorry.

8	It wasn't important.
OC	Then –
8	I was never going to find it. Not like it would've changed tomorrow.
	Y'know, I can't even remember what it was.
	Pause
OC	So, you going to cover the petrol then.
8	Is that a joke.
	OC gives her answer to the question MC asked in the car-game on p7.
	Pause
OC	Here, I thought of another one. *Life on Mars*.
8	What d'you mean?
OC	The ending.
8	Right.
OC	You look exhausted.
8	I'm good. I can play, but first –
OC	John Simm is in a meeting. What's he doing with his hand?
8	He's clicking a pen. Before we carry on –

OC and 8 recreate the ending of the TV-show 'Life on Mars'. The same note applies as for 'Thelma & Louise' in Scene One. See on p8

OC   [Police Officer] The case hangs on whether we have grounds to overturn the statute for violent cases. Press charges in forty-eight hours or release. Unless you can argue it will happen again. Plus, have that verified by –

8   The man carries on talking.

OC   But like it's underwater. We can't hear what he's saying.

8   We have to –

OC   The camera is on John Simm. He's spaced-out.

       [Police Officer] What's your feeling on this Sam? Sam?

8   [Sam] Oh. Sorry.

OC   [Police Officer] Do you think it's unethical to hold them longer than forty-eight hours, without pressing formal charges, when they may require a detailed evaluation?

8   He doesn't have an answer.

OC   The other people?

8   They're staring.

       [Sam] Um.

OC   He's holding this metal thing.

8	He's pressing it so hard into his thumb, he starts bleeding. It takes someone else –
OC	*[Police Officer]* Sam, stop. Look, your hand.
8	*[Sam]* I don't feel anything. Uh. Excuse me.
OC	The first note of the song you've been waiting the whole series to hear.
8	In 2006.
OC	This look comes over his face.
8	A revelatory kind of thing going on behind the eyes, like he's waking up to something.
OC	Like this strange episode –
8	Series of episodes.
OC	Is all starting to piece together.
8	He leaves the meeting.
OC	We see him on the roof.
8	He closes his eyes, lifts his head up to the sun.
OC	The song is loud now, the camera circles him.
8	He starts walking.
OC	In the direction of the edge.
8	His walk becomes a jog.
OC	Becomes a run.
8	The wind is picking up his jacket, his tie.

OC	He launches himself over the railing.
8	He jumps.
OC	We see him fall.
8	John Simm.
OC	Or his stuntman.
8	Waving his arms and legs.
OC	Black-out.
8	Alright, turn the car around.
OC	No, come on, there's still more: 1973, the train robbery, Gene Hunt.
8	We have something else to do. Turn around.
OC	What?
8	Go left.
OC	We're not going back, are we?
8	No. We're going forward. Straight on at the crossroads.
OC	That's not the way to your mum's.
8	Before that. We have hours yet.
OC	They use the time they have. They drive through her town, until they reach Newark and Sherwood Council building.
8	A new build. The security is lax. Not everything has been moved over yet.

OC	They slip in.
8	They find the records of last month's parking fines.
OC	They smuggle them out the building, underneath their clothes.
8	Drive to the Major Oak.
OC	And bury the papers at the base –
8	With Robin's forgotten loot.
OC	They break-in to the Capital One office in Nottingham city centre.
8	They remove hard-drives, un-plug servers, and delete cloud-storage.
OC	Set all credit card balances to zero.
8	Before the night is over –
OC	They write a sub-clause into British Law.
8	An amendment in red biro.
OC	That outstanding personal debts be forgiven.
8	If they haven't been paid back within eight years.
OC	They buy all the ad-space during day-time TV.
8	And fill it with static.
OC	Or play repeats of old sitcoms.
8	Or the music video for 'Bitch Better Have My Money'.

OC	They retire the elderly puppets from the Wonga adverts.
8	They replace the locks on vacant luxury flats.
OC	And hide fresh-cut keys under the mats of shelters and foreclosed homes.
8	They tattoo "CASH MY GOLD" on Dale Winton's forehead.
OC	They re-direct all payments on "amazon.co.uk" to Her Majesty's Revenue and Customs.
8	Until the full amount of Amazon's avoided tax is paid up.
OC	They take on the loan-books of the Debt Consolidation firms.
8	Close all accounts.
OC	They consolidate the debts into one lump sum, in their own names.
8	They cut their debt into chunks.
OC	Divide it up among several people.
8	All of them false identities.
OC	Aaron Adams through to Zelda Zychowski.
8	They keep splitting the debt into smaller pieces.
OC	Shared by more and more imaginary debtors.
8	Until each unit of debt is smaller than the smallest measure of currency.

OC   And it ceases to exist.

8   They do all of this.

OC   And all through the night she's thinking about
            her dad.

8   How it doesn't end, until you do.

OC   He took out a pay-day loan, when his boiler broke
            down. He ignored the water bill to pay it off. He
            thought it'd go away. He was tired of the cycle. He
            stuck his head in the sand, didn't open the letters,
            let them pile up on the mat and trod them into a
            mulch. Because there was never enough to put
            aside each month. And it's easier to think they'll
            forget about him.

8   Easier than it is to wake up in the morning and
            remember what's owed and not be able to act.

OC   It's only real when you answer the phone. The logic
            of the vulnerable.

8   He drew the curtains, put the TV on quiet. Took
            the batteries out the doorbell and the smoke alarm.
            Put on his coat, his jumpers and socks. Fed the cat
            first. Looked for loose tab ends on the pavement
            outside, when no one was looking. Waited for them
            to come, for them to knock on the windows and
            peer through the frosted glass, lift-up the letterbox
            and speak in loud but straight-forward voices. He
            didn't respond, he held his breath, moved the sofa
            away from the wall, lay down in the gap made
            between, and hid.

OC   And when they went, he poked his fingers out
            the letterbox. Stretched them wide. Felt the cold
            of the air. And he thought, if he left them there

long enough, the wolves might come, and eat him piece by piece. Starting with his fingers. Pull him through the slat. A way-out without a choice, without having to do it.

EPILOGUE

Stage Direction Four, turn to p.47

This is how it happened. More or less. In the space of a detour.

An improbable sequence of acts. We'll give you that.

We tell her story so many times, new plot-points creep in like weeds. Until the whole story is over-run and wild.

We tell her story as an exorcism. For unsettled ghosts and unsettled payments.

The story that comes after. One person, in a car. Re-joining an A-road and driving to a funeral. We won't show you the funeral. We'll give her some privacy. But we'll take you up to it. She arrives at her mum's house. She lets herself in and heads straight for the sofa, to close her eyes.

In the living room are her brothers. They should be sleeping. There's still hours until they're needed at the church. And they're already dressed. They've been trading places round the room. Re-tucking their shirts each time they stand up. Restless, desperate for something to do. And then: she arrives. And. They don't talk at first. They make sounds.

She takes the youngest in her arms and she holds him. The other two awkwardly wait their turn. These giant boys, trying to appear less big, less wanting, less in need. She pulls them in. They envelop her. Their breathing slows down. The start of what could become a cry. They stop themselves, they need to hang on. Not yet, not now. She yawns. She's so tired she breathes sleep, like a gas into the room. Within minutes they're all knocked out.

Their mum discovers them snoring. One of them is drooling. The boys' shirts are creased. But she doesn't mind that. She's in her dressing gown, and she's holding onto herself at the elbows. She thinks about taking a picture. Like the ones their dad used to take, the ones from when they were young.

NOTES ON PRODUCTION:

Stage Direction One

In the story, Main Character roots her hands around the hole in the floorboards. She looks for the object she's been seeking. She finds nothing.

In the performance, Performer One picks up a rucksack. She was wearing this during Scene One, and took it off at the start of Scene Two. She opens the bag and looks inside. She pulls out items you would find in an overnight bag – a toothbrush, a change of underwear, snacks, an energy drink. She gives up. She looks to the tech-desk. She looks backstage. We're not sure whether this is the actor or the character, whether someone has forgotten to pre-set the object in the bag. She looks in the bag again. She finds something. She pulls out another bag, identical to the first. She opens this bag, and empties out the same contents – toothbrush, change of underwear, snacks, an energy drink. And another bag. The same again. She speeds up. She becomes more desperate, as the Matryoska-Doll-like bags and their contents spill out across the stage. There are five bags in total, one for each scene in the show.

There are no doubt other ways to achieve this. What needs to be conveyed is that Main Character is looking for something that is not there, and perhaps never was. Ideally, this will involve a bit of slippage between character and performer, so that we're not sure whether the play has broken. What's important to capture is that everything changes, and the play spins off in another direction.

Stage Direction Two

In the story, 8-year-old strikes Main Character with a golf club, and kills her.

In the performance, when Main Character says "She's halfway down the stairs before I do anything", the LED strips (lining the front, left, and right of the stage) begin to alternate colours. They change colour when there is a change in who's speaking. Orange for 8-year-old and blue for Main Character. As we get further into the nightmare-like scene, the lights alternate faster and faster, no longer in accordance with a change in speaker. At the end of Scene Three there is a blackout, followed by full house-lights and 'The Court of the Crimson King' by King Crimson at a deafeningly loud volume. Performer Two picks up a pillow she'd been carrying when she entered Scene Three, and pummels Performer One with it. Feathers burst out of the pillow with each swing. Sometimes Performer One and Performer Two laugh. Sometimes they cry. Sometimes they scream. Once Performer Two has tired herself with swinging, she holds Performer One by the shoulders. King Crimson is still playing. Performer Two talks to Performer One. We can't tell what she's saying. What we see are two friends having an intimate conversation. They hug for some time. Performer One takes out the hoop-earrings she's wearing. Performer Two undoes Performer One's pony-tail, and puts Performer One's earrings into her own ears. Performer One sits down on the floor, with her head in her hands. In a snap, the music cuts, we return to a theatrical lighting state, and Scene Four begins.

There are many versions we tried here. We did a dance. A five-minute hug. A real-life fight. What we found the show needs is to sit the audience within a feeling, with the narrative on pause for a moment. The performers come together and the ownership of the story is handed from Main Character to 8-year-old. What we shouldn't see here is a choreographed piece of stage-combat in which one character hits another with a golf club.

Stage Direction Three

In the story, 8-year-old deconstructs her house. Years pass, and she gets filthy in the process.

In the performance, when 8-year-old says "Black tears run down the glass", Performer Two picks up a bottle of energy drink. This is one of the items that came out of the rucksacks in Scene Two. She takes a sip, and a thick black liquid dribbles down her chin. A pause. She holds back her head and pours the muddy contents over herself. She uses this action to drive forward through the monologue.

We always knew this moment should involve Performer Two getting dirty in some way. We knew she needed to be transformed, so we could see her shift from the 8-year-old to the Main Character. What's tricky is the placement. Maybe this moment should come earlier. Maybe it should come later, when she sets the house on fire. Maybe it shouldn't be fixed. But something definitely happens to show a gear-shift, a journey from one emotional state to another. It's up to you what happens and when.

Stage Direction Four

In the performance, the Epilogue was recorded as a voiceover. The performer speaking changes with each line-break. While this played over the speakers, Performer Two and Performer C open a hold-all. This had been brought on stage at the st the show, and had remained there unopened. Out of t Performer Two takes a towel to clean the mud off her two performers then remove a series of items - a nd brown boots, a faux-leather tunic, a green feather t of dress themselves to look like Robin Hood. The 'fancy-dress' about their appearance.

47